T0150085

# the

# blue-collar

# sun

# the
## blue-collar
# sun

lucas farrell

Printed in the United States

10 9 8 7 6 5 4 3 2 1

Green Writers Press is a Vermont-based publisher whose mission is to spread a message of hope and renewal through the words and images we publish. We will adhere to our commitment to preserving and protecting the natural resources of the earth. To that end, a percentage of our proceeds will be donated to social-justice and environmental activist groups. Green Writers Press gratefully acknowledges the generosity of individual donors, friends, and readers to help support the environment and our publishing initiative. For information about funding or getting involved in our publishing program, contact Green Writers Press.

Giving Voice to Writers & Artists Who Will Make the World a Better Place
Green Writers Press | Brattleboro, Vermont
greenwriterspress.com

Sundog Poetry Center, Inc.
www.sundogpoetry.org

isbn: 978-1-7336534-5-9

Excerpt(s) from *Under The Glacier* by Halldor Laxness, translated by Magnus Magnusson, translation copyright © 1972 by Magnus Magnusson. Used by permission of Vintage Books, an imprint of the Knopf Doubleday Publishing Group, a division of Penguin Random House LLC. All rights reserved.

Image credits: Book cover art by Emily Mason (1932-2019). Painting title is *From Space, 2018*, oil on canvas, 30 x 24 inches (76.2 x 61 cm), ©2020 Emily Mason and Alice Trumbull Mason Foundation/Artist Right Society (ARS), NY. Image courtesy of Christopher Burke.
Photos and drawings that appear on pages 62/63/64/66, as well as the author photo, are courtesy of Louisa Conrad, ©2020 Louisa Conrad.

Printed on recycled paper by Bookmobile. Based in Minneapolis, Minnesota, Bookmobile began as a design and typesetting production house in 1982 and started offering print services in 1996. Bookmobile is run on 100% wind- and solar-powered clean energy.

for louisa, always

& for maisie & minna, newly

More kindness will do nothing less
Than save every sleeping one
And night-walking one
Of us.

- James Dickey, "The Strength of Fields"

i

this is your animal

# ICE STORM

Everything in silver. The dog in the road. The two dogs in the road. The limbs of the trees enrobed. In silver. The sun in silver. The tongues of the lambs lapping ice limbs, silver. There is a music in the road that the dogs dog to. That the people people to. It's a dance I dance to. It's silver. It goes: who is this place, why did it home here, where's the beginning, now hurt me. There is an honest-to-god answer. I don't know what it is or where to find it, but I'm sensual to it. After all, we're not going to be here for very long. Stand arm in arm with the conditions and marvel.

# GERTRUDE GIVES BIRTH TO TWINS

To birth is to take in
fresher aspects of.
An owl's nest strewn
in a white field. My brother
coughing up sunlight
in a white field,
feathers. Five o'clock
half-grazes the snowed-in
shadows. Meaning, her kids
arrived here as into a flood.
As out of some liquid prayer.
O Gertrude, whose placenta
stretches clear
across this skyline:
I will listen listen listen
to all the unmurdered
birds. Singing in
the laboring heights.

# SUGARING

The snowy fields have softened to a raw chévre. I eat a little of it, I drink a little water, I sing a little mercy to myself. Fingers numb, I tune my ears to the 7 or 8 metal spouts in the vicinity dripping sap into tin amid a greater orchestra of uncertainty. Listen further, listen deeper: record the unkindnesses, the atrocities, bitter soliloquies, brutalities, note the sounds of the acts and the sounds of the consequences, and play them all back one by one on random on repeat in an empty wing of an underfunded museum in a thriving city somewhere in the vicinity of your heart and listen. Then reside there. Year after year for eighty some odd years, let's say a lifetime, let's call it life, call it weather, let's call it love.

# TWO PIECES OF DRIFTWOOD

Let them find us, years from now, washed of color,
eased of burden, elegantly perched side by side:
Two pieces of driftwood at rest in the high desert.
And when that day comes, in that ineluctable present,
let them falsely imagine that our journeys here
were straightforward. That our independent migrations
somehow synchronized. A history of wild togetherness.

But o god please also let them sense the truth of it.
A remote yet unmistakable, unhindered astonishment
at our having arrived here (together) at all.
At the impossibly boundless navigation of the heart.
For that is what this is. Impossible and possible.
A story with the same beginning, middle, and end:
Here we are. Here we are. Here we are.

# LANDSCAPING

For five whole minutes I tool with the weed trimmer.
Feed new line, snip, thread. Cap. Tighten. Thumb
the jellied prime more than is necessary.
Watch the bubble fill: a carbonated blue. Pull the starter
cord. Pull the starter cord again. Pull the starter cord
eight times, in succession, jesus, mary, and joseph, FUCK—
FUCK. FUCK. FUCK. FUCK. FUCK.
Curse the way my dad might've. Fail to recall with
precision his voice. Sit down. Breathe. Lower my back
to the earth. Dark clouds overhead spread like cancer.

# WILDFLOWERS

Casually        an acorn
births into the half-light
out of Fern's pursed anus

      Skids across the parlor floor

October 7th
6 a.m.
Through the window
leaves emulsify

      in the horizontal loin of
daybreak

A horticultural blue
awakens

Hurls the shape of an oak tree
at an oak tree

Horse flies pendulum

above a shit pile

I hear the horse flies, I smell the shit pile,
in that order

It's okay, I tell the goats,
Be easy —

wildflowers grow rampant

in the throats
of opera singers

# TENDING

What's it like being mammal. I half-expected the irresponsive donkey to bleed sap water from its haunches having moved on to the ethics of March. Mud Season. I insert the thermometer into the rectum. Press the little button. Wait six seconds. Look up. Try to source the chickadee's song. Trace the song to the branch of a sugar maple upon which sits: Nothing. Breathe. Listen. Like inventing the blues. Later on someone will tell me it's actually a red maple. Which one. Beep. 103.6. The sap is running like blue fish through a fresh dream. Danny says it's carrying a 3.4% sugar content, meaning 40 to 1. We all agree that sounds pretty like a face. What a day what with all these blessed actuals! The donkey rolls back onto her side but her gaze tangles up with the blue beyond. Meaning she's stuck with that far off look in her eyes. What's it like being mammal. Someone said it's like directing traffic in a dream. Like two birds perched on a limb in the dead of winter. One keeping itself alive by pecking flesh off the other. Sad story. The sap is running hard like a fat man on a treadmill. Come on, laugh a little. This whiskey tastes like deer breath.

# ORIENTEERING

Here's what I do: I take the present and try and focus on all the external phenomena in my immediate surroundings. Then I account for my not-so-immediate surroundings, maybe a nearby valley or body of water because the local is only local in relation to the version of the field reflected in the window I look at from the precise center of my grief. I want you egregiously. Define geography: you went away. Go away.

# THE STARS HERE AT THE FARM

THE STARS: What's it like being mammal?

MAMMAL: I've flattened the hay with the weight of my body to make it warm for the brown goat who is so incredible to be around.

LATER: I prayed for the first time in 18 months.

THE MAMMAL: In my vocabulary, an opera singer is someone you kiss after drinking wine for the better part of an afternoon.

LATER: I will pray for a stranger's health.  I will also pray for my own health.  I will say that I am, above all, very grateful for my blessings, which are not of my own devising.

SHE'S JUST SO INCREDIBLE TO BE AROUND: I can't tire out the seasons.  Oh yes you can, with a little yellow and some blue you pretty much can.

BROWN GOAT: I can't remember the last time I was truly pierced by the thought of a loved one dying, not actually being in the world anymore. The thought makes me—deciduously—very upset.

YELLOW: It betters me.

BLUE: I wish my memory had a better part of an afternoon.

THE WEIGHT OF MY BODY: There are 1000 ladybugs hatching inside my heart this very second, which is in the refrigerator, next to the Pellegrino.

THE STARS: I like you fine, handsome circle. I will touch you.

i approached
a little farewell

No reply?

I shivered and shook for a little while longer and looked hopelessly into the fog. Where am I?

But no reply. **No sign of life** in the house. At last my patience failed and I shouted out with all my strength of body and in this one word, **so** that the three sheep in a submarine... the house died away in terror.

Why?

The reply to this extraordinary shout was a dull... cry come out of the fog like that of a great black-backed gull... and across that. When **I listened more closely**... sounded by... as... I recognized it: it was the woman in the other house. She laughed and laughed. The noise I incited...

Now... crept away with his devil face in the middle of the laughter for too stiff in the silence... so... and... was a little frightened. When I was out of sight of the house I took to my heels with my heart flopping about inside me and ran **as hard as I could**... the tent I had come... ever imagining that I would find the man reading out...

The glacier the unconcealed of the world, arches over the

moves a tiniest fraction

towards the sea

The sound of birdcalls

a little out of practice

...to the sea... about five kilometers ahead, but the road is so twisting and climbs up and down so many glacier moraines that I was two hours all told on the road there and back.

The metropolis proved to consist of three farmsteads standing scattered at the frontier where the hill-road ends and the lava tongue above begins. In the cellar of one of the farms there was a tiny shop, and when I **finally** got hold of the farmer he could sell me from the shop's foodstocks some crab chocolate and tinned asparagus; and of course the celebrated Prince Polo biscuits, the only gastronomic luxury that Icelanders allow themselves since they became a wealthy nation. In the mouth the delicacy is not unlike the pumice one can find in dried-up riverbeds from the glacier, except for **a** little extra sweetness of taste that would make normal pumice rather more inedible than ever. Thereupon the undersigned forced down his tasty ration, as it says in the **poem about** Arinmundur of Krossbrunnur, for hunger was pressing hard. I sat on a grassy bank by the main road where a little brook ran past, and I had the brook along with the asparagus for dessert. The water was such that I never stood at last past the 100-Pumice-cold-water-drinking, which says that it's quite enough to have one hot time but not so just to eat it unless one is thirsty.

If I have forgotten to write about **the weather.** That is soon remedied: it has cleared up. A cloudless day. The glacier rises snowy-white and stock-still over an undisturbed priesthood who sits on a grassy bank by a brook chewing Prince Polo biscuits and is mentally arming himself to defend the revolution, the faith, and God's Christendom against conjurors, miracle-workers, horse-traders, and twelve-tonnet people. A good day. The day one did not lose one's faith. How precisely symmetrical the glacier is as it lies mirrored in the water of Bardarlaug.

and now in the box, probably had rather I pi not come. He was saying:

Good morning, pastor Jón.

Good morning.

Embla: So the fish can't book.

Pastor Jón had no comment to make on that.

Embla: Are you going off on a journey, pastor Jón?

Pastor Jón: I am waiting for a man who's giving me a lift.

Embla: Going far?

Pastor Jón: Over the mountain. The quick-freezing plant that is both out of order and bankrupt has now been given a subsidy of a million. They're going to try to start it up again. They asked me to help to repair the machinery. Jódínus is coming to fetch me.

Embla: Pastor, you know of course that Guðrún Sæmunds—don't you know?

Pastor Jón: Oh, did she say that was her name?

Embla: Haven't you met her?

Pastor Jón: Last a woman arriving late last night.

Embla: Do you really need to go away today? I have an idea the woman has come to see you.

Pastor Jón: By the way, have you had anything this morning?

Embla: Not very much, no. But it doesn't matter. I'm going with colds.

Pastor Jón: was see me from the stove and said: It's no good talking about her this with your mouth watering all day. I haven't had anything either, actually. But I've got some shark meat here. May I cut off you some?

Embla: I'm rather unaccustomed to shark meat, I've heard they it only.

Pastor Jón: Shark meat is the greatest delicacy in Iceland

good cause, that this churchyard had been abandoned for two years and that some practical joker had amused himself to using a place there and putting something or perhaps nothing into it. Perhaps there were some coarse youngsters from far districts at work, or some naughty children, or born people. It could well be right, as some people think — for the Madonna forgiveness was some other person altogether.

I was beginning to fear I could be bringing my superiors down south nothing but a book of dreams instead of a report from this mission to Glacier. It would make matters worse if one had to add a book of dream interpretations.

I tiptoed to the veranda of the bungalow to see if I could find any signs of something having happened. I saw none — a nice place — and became afraid. There is no more terrifying experience for a Christian than to discover he has suddenly become reasonable. The curtains were drawn in the windows just as the butler Jónas Smith had left them, no sign of any human habitation anywhere around the house as lead. Where were the great visitors? Vanished as if the earth had swallowed it. Merely a little bird flew down before on the veranda. But when I began to inspect the place more closely, I noticed the custom seal lying in a corner. The seal in other words had been broken, and scarcely in a decade. But who had broken it? Was it the woman? Or some other woman? Or some practical joker? What would Jútur Jónsen say about it?

When I was taking off the veranda again I came to notice a little something that in itself was hardly worth mentioning: one head-bone of a fish, picked clean, lying in front of the woman's door. Although the woman I had dreamt was perhaps not real, there had nonetheless whatever it was one was been a seal-fish lying on the veranda last night.

Christian observance is at a minimum in the district. In addition to the state of the church, there is the testimony of the postal clerk Jómi Jónsson of Brún, albeit given with sympathy and complete loyalty towards pastor Jón; **furthermore,** there is the interview with the clergyman himself, both on marked spools. From this documentary evidence it will be clear that clerical duties are hardly performed at all in the parish unless ministers from outside are called in; burials neglected, likewise taxes at Christmas, etc.

*Marital status.* Inquiries as instructed brought to light the following regarding pastor Jón's marital circumstances: was probably formally married, prefers to draw a veil over it, perhaps merely an empty formality, and *non consummatum*. The woman's name: various derivations from the word *Úsáli*; pastor Jón himself says the woman was called Úa. Happened, or rather didn't happen, thirty-five years ago. Who performed the wedding ceremony, if it was performed, not clear. Does the undersigned have the authority to require from a parish pastor an account of a private affair that has never been a matter of controversy within the parish or outside it, but that would certainly be a case for the police if taken up officially? Bigamy can hardly enter into it. Pastor Jón's unblemished life is common talk, together with the **love** and respect of the parishioners, probably unique. About the woman whom pastor H. has named his "bride" in the presence of the undersigned, the undersigned can only affirm she **is** from one of those ancient fishing places farther down the coast to the east that are more akin to ghost stories than reality; in these places live princesses of unusual physical characteristics that arise from the fact that they are **breast-fed by** wet nurses (perhaps no cows on the farms?) and that these women walk after **death, etc.** Both the

**We yearn to kill the**

**no longer visible**

May I call your attention to the fact that we are Lutheran here

Can't you see Don't you understand

You are bound to the ends of the

earth  Now I am going to touch you

**Where-
upon**

**daylight**

**heaved**

# Reality as the Head-Bone
# of a Fish

I took the underwater shots more to grasp for things in the darkening evening, and especially in wild circumstances of the shadows in these pictures. The shadows that were as gradually taken home, even by the wall of over solid shades was so huge that they are completely taken. These of it close me to the window was the marshal to be outside of the backside. Violent aggression accompanied to a storm that bore no relation to the actual night blowing so it was that I became accustomed to hearing from the cliffs through my sleep. If one looked out during the night at this time of year one would see one or two birds at the most, gliding past on some recorded errand. By complete contrast, there were now countless birds eddying and screaming over the homefield and the homefield. These were not big formations, but a few thousand some of the cliff colonies and go over black-backed gulls from

...

...reply. Thus we groped our way slowly through the drizzle far into the night.

After many attempts at **establishing** her position she finally found an insignificant side road that formed **a right angle with** the main road to the right. It was on sandy gravel. This side road, if it could be called a road, had been so little used that it was difficult to say whether it had ever had a vehicle over it, one could just make out some wheel tracks, but they could well have been natural... because in some places was... grass and... and over had had peace to grow on the road... ...side road that its... ... before... in the fog, at a time when **every bird in the land** ... ...

...

The woman looked at me and answered gently, "Where do you think this leads, except to the end of the world?"

And we continued to drive along the sandy gravel and tried to make out the track, but the fog reduced **the horizon** to three or four metres in front of the car.

After a while the landscape changed and this so-called road began to cross meadowlands pink with withered grass. Worst of all, the ground now **became** extremely soggy and this big car **nearly** three tons in weight, and low-slung, began to have diffi... ... ...

...he had the right to ... ... **unrecognisable** places at the ... ... And so it did. In the middle of... ...the engine cut out. When... ...the wheels sank, the back... ...

**By the way, who is**

**shooting**

**people** Instead of

**farming**

The light of the world

**might** as well tell you the truth:

**you**

*can turn the dark to light*

young man to stay the night with me. I'll make up a bed and
tidy up **the** living room. I'm going to **light** a fire. Then I **shall**
bake you some bread. Do please have a seat on the wall of the
vegetable garden while you wait, my dear.

The **house** was unlocked and she opened the door and went
straight in with her case and closed **the** door behind her.

The vegetable garden had not been dug, yet and the dog had
probably been hanged, because often sheep were besieging the
house. Under the farmhouse wall there stood a thicket of wil-
low, birch, and angelica all intertwined, growing above the
high **withered** grass; the old people had not had the energy to
restore the fence, so the sheep cropped the leaves as soon as
they sprouted. A ewe looked at me severely from under the
thicket and bleated accusingly.

When I had hung about for a while out in the night, I had
started wondering what the woman had meant when she whis-
pered that we were going to the end of the world. Was it this
place?

My fingers were so stiff I could hardly get my shoes on.
What had become of the woman? Was she having so much dif-
ficulty in waking the old couple? Or was it so hard to get their
consent for a young man to stay the night with her? There was
no smoke coming from the chimney, either. Warm bread still
seemed a long way off. Soon I had started shivering. Was I to
perish of cold here—or what was I to do? Perhaps the best solu-
tion to the problem would have been to open the door, walk in,
and go straight into the bed of the warm woman. Unfortu-
nately no brilliant ideas occurred to me. I could not keep quiet
and shouted in the direction of the house:

Where are you?

...I have only one theory, ...it will save the world...

that men worship are equally good. In the Bhagavad Gita
which pastor Jon cites, Krishna is reported as saying, as I recall:
You are free to **address** your prayers to any god at all, but the
one who answers the prayers, I am he. Is this what pastor Jon
means when he says that all gods are equally good except the
god that answers the prayers, because he is nowhere? So the God of
these two standpoints can be accommodated within the same
work of our confession of faith. The god who speaks through
Krishna's words isn't particularly pleasant, either, because he
alone controls the card-game and **the other** gods are only dum-
mies, and he is the one who declares on their cards. At any rate,
this god is rather far removed from the seventy-year-old grand-
father **with** the large beard who came to breakfast with Father
Abraham of Ur, accompanied by two angels, his attendant,
and settled in with him, and whom the Jews inherited and
thereafter the pope and finally the Saxons. When Krishna says
he is the one god who answers prayers, then this is truly not just
our orthodox god of the catechism, the one who says: I am the
Lord thy God, thou shalt have no other gods before me. Pastor
Jon says, on the other hand: Thou shalt have all other gods
before the Lord thy God. What is the answer to that?

But theology apart, people here at Glacier joke about the
fact that whenever pastor Jon travels from farm to farm on his
mare he is pursued by herds of **free-range** horses and flocks of
snow buntings and even ravens, because he keeps their cus-
toms to food. The ethical code that moulds pastor Jon is best
seen to be found, perhaps, in the **compassion** theology of the
twelfth century.

*Concerning a funeral on Snæfellsjökull.* Whether this funeral
took place behind the church's back or to some extent with its
connivance, the parish pastor has nothing to say. The parish

he had forgotten his name. He quite responded when I called him. When I barked he came to me, right enough, but he didn't know me. **I am** a bride like that dog.

Embi: Forgive me if I don't entirely agree with the comparison that I've applied to yourself, pastor Jón. You remind me rather of those blissful people in religious paintings—the ones who smile while they are **being hacked to pieces**. In other respects, I wouldn't dream of contradicting what you say.

Pastor Jón: Sometimes I feel it's too early to use words until the world has been created.

Embi: Hasn't the world been created, then?

Pastor Jón: I thought the Creation was still going on. Have you heard that it's been completed?

Embi: Whether the world has been created or is still in the process of being created, must we not, since we are here, to one another in that strange dissonance called human speech? Or should we be silent?

Pastor Jón: You must not think I am asking the bishop's representative... First, I merely think that words, words, words and the Creation of the world are two different things, two incompatible things. I do not see how the Creation can be turned into words, let alone letters, hardly even a fiction. History is always entirely different to what has happened. The facts are all fled from you before you start the story. History is simply a fact on its own. And the closer you try to **approach** the facts through history, the deeper you sink into fiction. The greater the care with which you explain a fact, the more nonsensical a fable you fish out of chaos. The same applies to the history of the world. The difference between a novelist and a historian is this, that the former tells lies **deliberately** and for the fun of it,

# Philosophy at Glacier

We seem to have entered into philosophic conversation. My soul progresses quicker in philosophy than in all other things when you are dead inside your coffin, but instead you are collecting of the lilies of the field, and also getting you closer to a closer state of communication, compassionate, and a pure revelation as well.

Parlor four: It's a privy session to talk about one another's minds. Words are misleading. I am always trying to forget words. That is why I contemplate the lilies of the field, but in particular the glacier. **If one looks at the glacier** for long enough**, words cease to have** any **meaning** on God's earth.

Parlor Dorris: Is it that language needs divorced all at once, or do we merely reject?

Pastor Jón: I once had idea that someone needs to forget...

... I approached ... a little farewell ... a little broken-voiced sound, like ... a children's concertina ... that ... this ... Glacier should come to an end, ... that ...

It ... should ... express ... the ... history ... of ... seeing and having seen. The report has not just become part of my ... blood— ... my life has fused into one with the report. ...

We'll wade home through the

shiny black

opening

in    the

outcome

iii

# the blue-collar sun

Thinking how the strands of love convolute.
How the strands of love plead their diffidence,
wince at the blinding teat of the sun, which is yellow,
which is yellow. I've been in love with you since 7.

It is now 8:30 in the p.m. I guess you could say I'm committed.
Listen: The sound of a creek bed, bone-dry and motherless,
silences, like a spider, its capture. Seasonally.
Love's furious lines of latitude unreel,

thereby honoring the occasion of first light.
We can't wait for the next choice phenomenon to appear:
the bare-chested clouds. The bare-chested moon.
An éventail of empathy that the blue-collar sun,

that the blue-collar sun drags above the screen. Rises,
unforgiving. How it gives and it gives with its bare hands.

Like fireflies we excused ourselves
horizontally through the fields.

Vendors of hearts in the stadium of night.

I used to think the bird migrating
through my memory was the lone offender. My mother's
was an arctic tern whereas mine was a common snow
goose. Each time an explosion sounds, another wing
retires to the field.

We tell time by the habits of a greater
falling.

I've spent my life detecting, with
increasing difficulty, the reverberant thump, my
scalpel scabbed over, eft-red, having stabbed at the
rain, having scalped it. When I perform the little
surgeries, she calls me miraculist. Then we set the
hearts in glass boxes and seek out the buyers. She
calls our line of products see-throughs.

At night I hold onto her so I don't lose
myself to the Shoulder Elvis.

The fields are overgrown, they're six feet tall.

I used to think my bird would not get lost
but now I don't.

The world is hard to find once you start
looking for it.

It's hard to tell anything when it's just me.
When I'm the lone offender.

But she is with me. She calls me a textbook
gamester. A Windham County felon. A regular snow goose.

To think the bird would lose its way.

We hold on to each other and the fields spin
round like pinching the nose and blowing your lights out.

It's midnight. You can tell by the erratic
sway of the paraplegic moon. It's in its
numb-from-the-hips-up phase.

O god where is the textbook on living.

We measure the heights from which the
hearts fall and she charts the results in her planner.
The fields at this hour pulse prophetic like the lungs of
venting hens. Like the surprise side streets of the moon.

The old man was our very first buyer. He's
the one told us if the bird's thump resounds skyward
before the echo of the explosion subsides, we should
consider ourselves on the right side of luck.

There's a misfortune in the eyes of the dead
but not the dying.

I used to think it was the other way around
but who can say. One lacks the element of surprise
whereas the other migrates north according to the angle
of its encounter with light.

I am a man. How can life not be happening
to me, too. I go on pat-drying the sweaty temples of the
blue-collar sun with a rag I can't keep clean. At night I
hold onto her like a seeing eye dog. We invigilate each
other's breathing like fields of tall handsome men. O
won't they just love me and think of me. In my dream I
come upon the girl cradling the migrating bird and my
grip on the scalpel slackens and shudders.

O this is a serious thing.

Up north we can hear, when the winds bed
down, the apologetic wheeze of the righteous.

We haven't encountered a buyer in weeks.
It's a job trying to keep the days straight. Some make a
career of it, I do. I dream the bird is mine and my faith
splits through the seams of god's whiteknuckled fist.

Staining the hardwood floors of night.

The next buyer's blindness was white as leek root. White like the sorest strep throat in America. White white white white white.

Hallelujah.

Stung like Braille the newborn hand.

A young woman from the Midwest whose default mode was that of flattery. Young enough to plant a garden for. I told her what do you call a moth this big.

A bird.

Haha.

She carried away two days' worth. The explosions occur in unison only on the solstice. Love minus the weather. Two negatives make a positive, isn't that just the heights? I never know if it's the moon eclipsing the sun or what.

The moon steadies a firefly between its front teeth. Arcs forth a flickering loogie. Floors a stand of New England hardwoods.

There's a certain regionalism that inheres despite intentions. Remember that. Gestures betray. For instance, males of one species of firefly mimic the flash patterns of another so as to pat-dry the sweaty temples of the beautiful rival.

Hope you can hear me.

The next buyer we encountered was a mechanic. His grease rag was like mine only it had a red stripe run lengthwise across it like a row of apple trees athwart a distant hill. He was my mother's mechanic.

O the bird was on some kind of course, alright.

When my girl greeted him her voice caved in and the grass some ten feet away sneezed and shook. Swayed like the back of a clockmaker's eyelid. Pendulous blindspots. We stopped and looked for whatever it was but there was nothing.

Silence.

I could hear the ringing in my mother's ears, what she called her Shoulder Elvis.

The mechanic's name was Bob. He possessed the nonchalance of a seeing eye dog, which never failed to give me pause even as a grownup. You can't outgrow reactions. You can only account for them with increasing difficulty whereas birds can be taught migration. By the same token, it is known that older birds are more successful wind correctors and therefore.

A bird's heart resembles a human's but is slightly larger in relation to its body size. The fields of New England resemble those out west save for the fireflies.

What do you call a firefly this big I asked
him.

Run!

Haha.

Before we sold the Buick I'd accelerate to
eighty along a dirt road out of town, alongside a field of
wetland fern, eighty-five, ninety, and suddenly the
lanterns would smear horizontal, blur and bend hell-bent
on astronomy.  Then, at a certain speed, on a moonless
night, those astral smears would begin to circle back in
on themselves.

It's hard to know what to do with myself.

How to live and in which direction.

A bird's heart, like that of a human's, has
four chambers and an ascending aorta.

A bird's pumping is slightly accelerated due
to a heightened metabolism.

Nautical-twilight fierce.

The science of it all so impressed the
mechanic that the stretch of landscape within reach of
his energy field went berserk.

I believe the blind can experience mirages
greater or equal to.

Look, sometimes we know what others are
thinking even before they do. Like leaving a weather
report on your gravestone because, hell, anything can be
predicted.

And sometimes the other is you which I
think about a lot actually, I think it's wild.

The solstice realigns twice a year and when
that happens the girl and me we hold onto each other the
way we hold onto each other's failures.

Which is neither fair nor amendable.

Anyhow, when her voice caved in and the
mechanic smiled, I watched his gold teeth converse with
the sun which was stinging the eastern sky like the
spanked rear end of a child.

That's when I knew how many years we'd
shared.

The bird was on some kind of course alright.

White white white white white.

Finally the damn turkey ten feet over
reared its head just above grassline like a floretless
flower, like a black-eyed susan.

My girl was lightheaded so I handed her the
bottle of milky water which was nearly full though it was
late afternoon again which meant we were
dehydrated-ascetic. She took it and put it to her lips.

Sometimes we don't have to speak at all to know what the
other has been meaning to say all his or her life.  That's
a certain candidness about experience I've come to
appreciate.  That and watching the birds we've saved
disappear behind some low-lying cloud thereby revealing
what our love stands in relation to.

Go like that with your.

Now with your eyes like when you're a kid.

Make two of anything like take for example
this field this heart.

The Shoulder Elvis sure is turned up
volumetrically by the buzzing life of these acres.

Listen.

There's some augmentation going on which
she took note of in her planner.  She handed me a look that
said I know about you and cicadas, how they make you
think of bathtubs.  And how bathtubs make you
subsequently think far too intently on your mother, each
night carrying pots full of boiling water from the stove
in the kitchen to the black porcelain tub out in the yard.
Did you hear what was firstly brought manmade into space.
Left it bobbing indelibly through the void.

A birdbath by god.

Yes, the bird that migrates through memory has about it a blackness and a roundness. Think: an overripe cherry in the throat of a robin. En route from the lower esophagus to the born-again tree. Like how these old philosophers went from conjecturing a flat earth to a round one. Via negativa. When I think about that with my body, my posture stiffens.

The turkey went lost to the thicket.

The mechanic was so impressed by the anatomy of his bird, by the very specifics of its living, of its having lived and died, the whole nine-thousand yards of it, that the landscape surrounding us went berserk. That's how hard he was trying not to show what certainty meant to him.

The sun slid on its blue collar, which is another way of saying the sun rose, and I could see again, o couldn't we just see the sad lot of it.

The old man was the first buyer and that was before we knew we were selling anything, period. He gave us a year's worth which changed everything instantly. I quit my job at the service station, gave back the costume but not the grease rag.

In class I told my teacher and everybody else too that my special talent (because that's all they want to know) was not dissolving in the bathtub.

Which was a quote I stole from Pablo Picasso. And here I was again thieving it to the mechanic, as well.

My girl smuggled me a look that said, I know what you're up to, you're fixing it so that this time next week that mechanic is going to realize the green depth of your persuasion.

Okay.

We sold him a couple of hen's hearts, a mourning dove's, a stellar jay's.

And in accordance with the memory of my mother, I offered up the heart of an arctic tern.

I spoke to him the details and she supplied the measurements which upped the monetary value, don't believe otherwise.

There is the old habit of a greater falling gleaned in the eyes of the sun that is rising, and in the steadying eyes of the winged.

On account of man's ambition.

Try identifying with that kind of sadness.

Like how if we put our minds to it we can feel, can actually feel the ache of tern teeth, the migrating ones, which endlessly travel, from pole to pole, twice a year, grinding the light. They see and taste more of that blue-collar sun than any other living creature, period.

See it all the more clearly with their eyes closed.

I asked the mechanic if I could fold his grease rag into a square, o won't you just give me this one thing.

Won't you love me and think of me.

The red stripe was thin as the heart's brakepad.

Delicate as tickling a moth's back. Like lulling it in the direction of some plywood dream.

It was clear by the way the creases took a backseat to the wrinkles that this man never kept his rag folded the way I liked to.

Never mind all that.

I put my face to it and gauzed a quick prayer and felt the sun eyeing me. I inhaled for the sake of the dissolved many. I folded it into a square.

There is a certain kindness in all buyers is what I believe. Mother taught me that by way of her grievances.

Some see us for who we are, too.

Which is a certain candidness about life etc.

Bob gave the girl and me a month's worth. I was to learn all this afterwards. Via the girl's calculations.

Giving is like that, isn't it, she said. It's clementine strange.

I used to think she gave herself too hard a time about certain things but now I don't which worries me like maybe I don't love her as much.

I hope that's just how life is and not how I am.

And yet she's the only reason I go on doing what I do. Conveying the value of the fallen. The quality of our ability to love. Otherwise the bird winging through my memory would fear not the darkness but would substantiate its claims over these fields and get the hardwon-actual buzzing electric, like the fireflies of New England, like mother's Shoulder Elvis, like the peeling back of that old adhesive sun from newly vacant stretches of the sky.

I told him o o o I can write the pants off an
obituary

& then the weather held up some recourse
where the joke should've been

& the fireflies are mingling like it's the
Stone Age / like it's the girl with no hands inventing fire
for the first time by rubbing the air real fast (the air
that occupies the absence)

Like a blind man describing a sunset to a
blind man and/or to a sunset:

SUCH A THIN, LABORIOUS ARC

Have you ever seen anything so beautiful
she says (so help me god, I haven't)

For in the middle of all that darkness
stands a cathedral, a cathedral that is itself spilling
darkness, & in the middle of that cathedral, amid all
that inner darkness, she's got her hands like this, and
above her hands, though you can't quite make it out, is a
mouth, an ordinary mouth, and right this very second in
time, at precisely this spot on the planet, here in this
very existence that we share without regard to the
impossibility of it all, of the world's being here, of our
being here, of our being here TOGETHER, that singularly
expressive mouth is formulating some gratitude, is
meaning to say, I did this for you / so help me / I did all
of this / for you

iv

a description of the
hook i am capable of

I WAS GIVEN THIS HOOK TODAY. A fish hook. And so it is lying flat on my desk. It appeared yesterday on the bottom of the boot that Louisa wears on her foot when she goes places. Usually she is walking, but not always. This was on one of those occasions when she was walking, walking around this town which is relatively small but also relatively big. Most of its citizens are relatives of one another. We are relative too, in that we happen to be walking through. And not just walking through but also not walking through. As in, staying the night. Several nights. A month. Which is also to say that we are living here. Living in a modest room with a bed and a small drawer for dirty clothes and nothing more in a shared house with windows some of which open and others that don't and also six sinks. But we are not just living in a room in a house in a town. Because to say living is also to say being. This hook was being itself but also not being itself when it pierced the boot Louisa wears on her foot when she goes places even when I am not with her. Clung to it. Was one of the fisherman's hooks. Is also to say it belongs partly to everyone in town. Because everyone in this town is related to a fisherman. Actually, if I'm not mistaken, this town is a village. A fishing village. Which means that everyone is either a fisherman or is related to a fisherman. Louisa is related to both the fishermen and also to the fish now that she has stepped on a hook that itself already belonged to a set of relationships; that is, existed among a set of relations. And so she too has become related and is therefore partly to blame. That's the long of it.

The short of it is that this hook is now lying flat on my desk whereas yesterday it was stuck to Louisa's boot and before that not lying flat but rather dragging vertically through the Atlantic and before that attached to the end of a monofilament line, pinched between the pink fingers of a fisherman, and before that was in the mouth of a fish whose blood smatters the hands one shakes in greeting when one comes to live in a village like this one. Or when one stays in such a village. Or when one is merely walking through. And it is not just haddockblood that smatters the hands one shakes in greeting. It is also codblood. And catfishblood. And birdblood. Because it just so happens that the fishermen in this village also shoot birds. With guns.

And just yesterday around five o'clock which is when Louisa likes to go places and take pictures of those places especially as they exist at a certain time of day, namely five o'clock, Louisa said she wanted to go places and to take pictures of those places and I understood her to mean time. And I often accompany her because it often occurs that at 5 o'clock I feel like walking away after a whole day of not walking away. And so yesterday I accompanied her. And we found ourselves both going places and walking away at 5 o'clock. And before we knew it we were walking along the shore of the Atlantic. And we kept on walking to where a band of old warehouses was once erected to serve a particular function they no longer serve. And in that way, they are just like the hook.

The short of it is that these warehouses used to process a kind of fish that is no longer fished here. And not just here, but anywhere really. And though there are many varying opinions held among the people who live in this village as to why this happens to be the case, it seems

clear, at least to me, that the lack of presence of this
kind of fish in this part of the world and also anywhere
really is not due to a superabundance of misplaced
hooks but is rather due to all these fish being dead.
Which itself results in a superabundance of hooks. That
is, a surplus of hooks. Therefore, a hook that goes
missing in a village such as this, in a time such as ours,
isn't actually considered lost. Isn't considered period.

But let us consider it nonetheless.

The long of it would be to say that this hook is now lying
flat on my desk in this studio which is itself just one of
those old warehouses whose purposes have been
reenvisioned on account of the kind of fish that is no
longer being caught anywhere in the living world: the
dead kind. And so the hook belongs to an old set of
relations that is both alive and not alive and also
belongs to a new set of relations. And if Louisa was to
take a picture of the hook I would say okay, that is fine,
there it is, but please also take, if you wouldn't mind, a
picture of its time.

And now having said that, I'd like to take a minute to describe to you the varying sets of relationships which I think I am capable of describing and yet also not capable of describing. Which is fine, actually. You're still going to go on walking and not walking and living and being whether you've read this description or not and you're still going to go on dying whether you've read this description or not and, frankly, so will I. One thing that's certain is that most of the time I don't feel the urge to write about fish. Not anymore. There was a time when Louisa was taking pictures of the Pacific salmon on the coast of Oregon and I happened to be with her because even then we enjoyed going places together and so I saw just how tremendously sad and also how tremendously beautiful the salmon's falling apart was. Because you see, a Pacific salmon's body will actually physically disintegrate, one hunk of soft flesh at a time, in the act of procreation. It's called spawning. And when the last hunk of soft flesh falls from the salmon it is very confusing as to what becomes of this salmon. Because the soft hunks of flesh actually nourish the offspring, welcoming them into the living world.

And so you can see why I wanted to write about the salmon of Oregon. But now I don't think I am capable of a task as tremendously difficult as that. And so I'd rather write about this hook. Okay. I will write about this hook, which looks more or less like this:

So like I was saying Louisa and I were walking down by the old fish processing warehouses when we came upon a casual heap of newly dressed and vacant-looking birds with eyes sprung open wide

not on account of the uncompromising
splendor of the polar sky  at 5 o'clock

or even the curious strangers
standing before them in such proximity — strangers who
were themselves surprised to see so many creatures meant
for the sky lying in a tangle upon a very warm heap — but
rather because of death. The eyes of the birds were open
wide on account of their being dead.

There was no question about that. Not anymore. And their bodies were limp and their feathers damp and muddied and their necks unnaturally contorted on account of their having been newly dressed and quartered.

The man, a fisherman, was still dressing and quartering more of these birds not ten feet away. We looked up. He was a very kind man and he even nodded enthusiastically and not impatiently when Louisa said can I take your picture and even was nice enough to — and i could tell he was proud and also a gentle man and also not so gentle and probably happy and also not so happy — hold up a bird proudly and even to reach out his thick arm to place a blood smattered hand on the shoulder of his grandchild so as to pull the boy in close for the purposes of the picture. For his grandchild was learning and also experiencing the virtues of boyhood and relativity and so on. And they both took hold of a wing and held the bird up and the man smiled and the boy looked tough and the bird looked dead. And the boy was wearing glasses and galoshes that looked a little bit like my galoshes which I bought for seven dollars six years ago in a place altogether different from this one in case I would one day get to go to a place altogether different from that one, so that I might wear them once I got there.

And after posing for Louisa, who was no longer as
concerned about taking pictures of places and/or time,
the kid went back to stomping shyly

on the neck of the most recently dressed bird, which explained why the necks of the birds in the heap were so unnaturally contorted and also explained the noise: the pulpy, hollow, abrasive, repetitive, flatsoda squishing and soft soft stamping of the neck muscles between the cement of the sidewalk and the boy's rubber bootbottom. That warm, textured noise that Louisa and I could hear almost as far back as the village. A wet and seductive noise.

A song.

So the fishermen in this village also happen to shoot birds. It is not surprising. Actually it is quite commonplace this far north, especially in the remoter regions, but also elsewhere too, in places neither remote nor northerly. That is, the shooting of birds by fishermen for the sake of their livelihood is nothing to get worked up about. No. It is like having a post office and also a different place where you go to mail your letters to loved ones when they go places and you don't go places anymore because you don't want to go away. It wouldn't make sense. Nor would it make any difference to the pure understanding of what a person is capable of and also what that person is not capable of.

Because you don't want to go away anymore. And so you are almost living, which is to say living and also not living. And if you are almost living then you are also almost being. And there is a description of this hook which I am capable of and also a description I am not capable of.

You are almost being yourself as a result of your not wanting to go away anymore.

Because it is now Tuesday and it is also 5 o'clock and I see that I too am part of a new set of relations that I don't want to walk away from. There is both the knowing that if I did walk away then I wouldn't know what else to do with myself and then there is also the question of not being sure I could possibly bear finding myself among one more set of relationships. Because when there's a first one, then by definition there's a second one. And probably there's even another one after that. And another. And then another one and another one and another one and another one and another one and another one and another one and on and on and on like that all your life. And then there isn't another one. Because that's your last one.

And after being here all day and not wanting to walk away anymore I am capable of also knowing that what I am not wanting to walk away from is being here. And if Louisa wants to go places because it is 5 o'clock and she feels like going places and taking pictures of those places and also of time and will even go without me, well, that's just life. Because if you want to, you can be a fisherman. And if you want to, you can be a fisherman that also shoots birds for the sake of his livelihood. And if you want to, you can be a fisherman who shoots birds and has a grandson who is looking tough and is not smiling and who is beginning to realize just how related he is to everyone in the village and in the post office and in the house with six sinks and to everyone else and to every living thing really who happens to be gentle and not gentle and happy and not happy and alive and not alive and tremendously alive.

## Acknowledgments

"Two Pieces of Driftwood" was written for Abe Streep & Stephanie May Joyce to mark the occasion of their wedding.

Thank you to Lily Brown for first publishing "Gertrude Gives Birth to Twins" and "Ice Storm" in *RealPoetik*.

"Sugaring," "Wildflowers," and "Orienteering" first appeared in *Poetry Northeast.*

Thanks and appreciation to Amber Nelson, who first published the section entitled "the blue-collar sun" as a chapbook by *Alice Blue Books*.

"i approached a little farewell" is composed of a series of erasures of pages derived from the novel *Under the Glacier* by Halldor Laxness, translated by Magnus Magnusson, and used by permission of Vintage Books, an imprint of the Knopf Doubleday Publishing Group, a division of Penguin Random House LLC. Many of these poems were originally paired with photographs by American visual artist, Louisa Conrad, and were exhibited at the Freies Museum in Berlin, Germany, as part of a show entitled "To The Thawing

Wind." Special thanks to the curator of that show, Emilie Trice.

"a description of the hook i am capable of" was first published in *DIAGRAM* , and was written while living at an artist residency in northern Iceland, in the town of Skagaströnd. At the time, Louisa was working on a series of ink & blood drawings of Icelandic cod on vellum--a provocative assembly-line of feverish little elegies. And our shared studio was in an old herring (síld) factory, first erected in the 50s or 60s, prior to the devastating collapse of that species. Louisa was also documenting the 5 o'clock sky on a daily basis--the seasonal "disappearance" of light--with the help of her Roloflex. It was during one of these outings that she discovered a hook piercing her boot-bottom.

I am and will be forever grateful to Mary Ruefle.

An enormous thank you to Sarah Audsley and Neil Shepard of the Sundog Poetry Center for all the good work that they do, and for their kindness, encouragement, and editorial guidance.

Thank you to Dede Cummings of Green Writers Press.

The cover art is a painting entitled "From Space, 2018" by the late Emily Mason, a dear friend and a gifted painter whose work and life are a continuing source of inspiration for me and for many. A special thanks to Mel Kahn, Steven Rose, and the other board members at the Emily Mason and Alice Trumbull Mason Foundation for permission to use the painting.

Love and thanks to my parents, Thomas and Deborah Farrell, and to Whit and Ellen Conrad.

Finally, thank you to Louisa Conrad, my companion in love and art and goat farming and parenting and LIFE.

Lucas Farrell lives in Vermont, where he and his wife own and operate Big Picture Farm, a small hillside goat dairy and award-winning farmstead confectionery. His first book of poems, *The Many Woods of Grief* (University of Massachusetts Press), was awarded the Juniper Prize for Poetry. He has two daughters.